D

LOOK INSIDE
CROSS-SECTIONS
SHIPS

ILLUSTRATED BY
JONOTHAN POTTER

WRITTEN BY
MOIRA BUTTERFIELD

DK

DORLING KINDERSLEY
LONDON • NEW YORK • STUTTGART

A DORLING KINDERSLEY BOOK

Art Editor Dorian Spencer Davies
Designer Sharon Grant
Senior Art Editor C. David Gillingwater
Senior Editor John C. Miles
U.S. Assistant Editor Camela Decaire
Production Ruth Cobb
Consultant John Robinson
The Science Museum, London

First American edition, 1994
2 4 6 8 10 9 7 5 3
Published in the United States
by Dorling Kindersley Publishing, Inc.,
95 Madison Avenue, New York, New York 10016

Library of Congress Cataloging - in - Publication Data

Butterfield, Moira, 1961-
Ships / written by Moira Butterfield;
illustrated by Chris Lyon and Jonothan Potter. – 1st American ed.
p. cm. – (Look inside cross-sections)
Includes index.
ISBN 1-56458-521-2
1. Naval architecture – Juvenile literature.
2. Ships – Charts, diagrams, etc. – Juvenile literature.
3. Seafaring life – Juvenile literature.
[1. Ships. 2. Seafaring life.]
I. Lyon, Chris, ill.
II. Potter, Jonothan, ill. III. Title. IV. Series.
VM150. B88 1994
623. 8'2 – dc20   93 – 46382
                                            CIP
                                            AC

Reproduced by Dot Gradations, Essex
Printed and bound by Proost, Belgium

CONTENTS

TRIREME

6-7

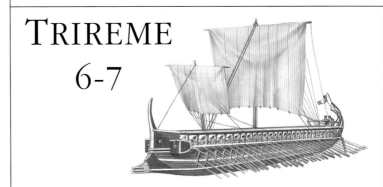

MARY ROSE

8-9

MAYFLOWER

10-11

HMS PANDORA

12-13

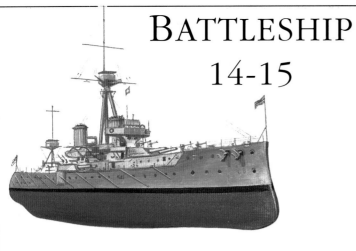

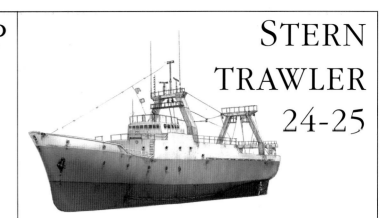

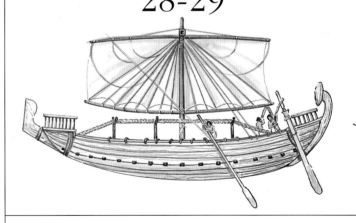

TRIREME

IMAGINE A FLEET of fast, narrow ships coming toward you, each one painted with a set of fearsome eyes on the front. You would hear the splashing of oars and see swords glinting in the sun. If you were an enemy, the sight would fill you with fear. You would be facing a trireme. Triremes belonged to the powerful nation-state of ancient Athens about 2,400 years ago. As yet, no one has found any remains of a trireme. However, it's possible to figure out what they looked like by studying pictures on ancient Greek vases and carvings, and a trireme reconstruction has recently been built.

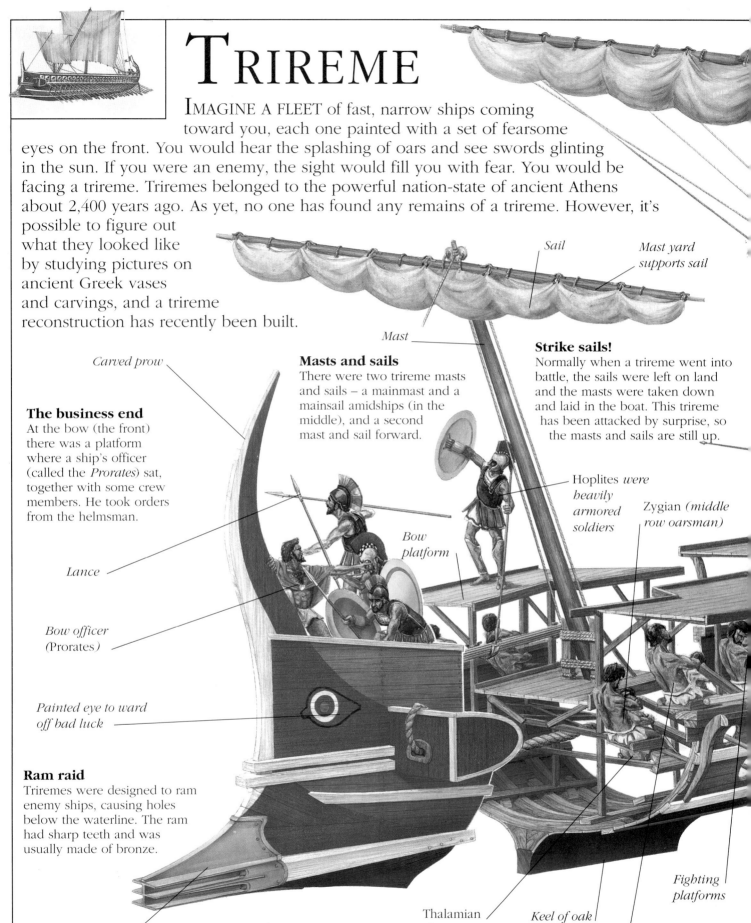

Sail

Mast yard supports sail

Mast

Masts and sails
There were two trireme masts and sails – a mainmast and a mainsail amidships (in the middle), and a second mast and sail forward.

Strike sails!
Normally when a trireme went into battle, the sails were left on land and the masts were taken down and laid in the boat. This trireme has been attacked by surprise, so the masts and sails are still up.

Carved prow

The business end
At the bow (the front) there was a platform where a ship's officer (called the *Prorates*) sat, together with some crew members. He took orders from the helmsman.

Lance

Bow platform

Hoplites *were heavily armored soldiers*

Zygian (middle row oarsman)

Bow officer (Prorates)

Painted eye to ward off bad luck

Ram raid
Triremes were designed to ram enemy ships, causing holes below the waterline. The ram had sharp teeth and was usually made of bronze.

Fighting platforms

Underwater ram

Danger! Splinters!
There were 170 oarsmen on board, each pulling a heavy oar. They rowed in time to music played by a piper.

Thalamian (bottom row oarsman)

Keel of oak wood

Thranite (top row oarsman)

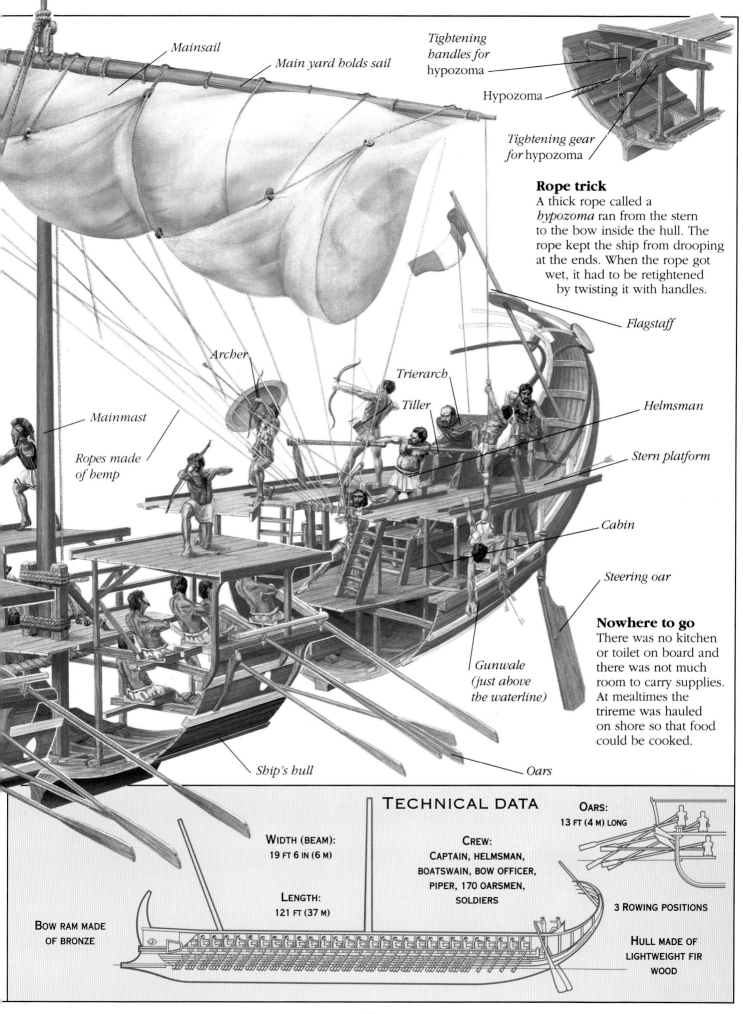

Mainsail

Main yard holds sail

Tightening handles for hypozoma

Hypozoma

Tightening gear for hypozoma

Rope trick
A thick rope called a *hypozoma* ran from the stern to the bow inside the hull. The rope kept the ship from drooping at the ends. When the rope got wet, it had to be retightened by twisting it with handles.

Flagstaff

Archer

Trierarch

Tiller

Helmsman

Mainmast

Ropes made of hemp

Stern platform

Cabin

Steering oar

Nowhere to go
There was no kitchen or toilet on board and there was not much room to carry supplies. At mealtimes the trireme was hauled on shore so that food could be cooked.

Gunwale *(just above the waterline)*

Ship's hull

Oars

TECHNICAL DATA

WIDTH (BEAM): 19 FT 6 IN (6 M)

LENGTH: 121 FT (37 M)

CREW: CAPTAIN, HELMSMAN, BOATSWAIN, BOW OFFICER, PIPER, 170 OARSMEN, SOLDIERS

OARS: 13 FT (4 M) LONG

3 ROWING POSITIONS

BOW RAM MADE OF BRONZE

HULL MADE OF LIGHTWEIGHT FIR WOOD

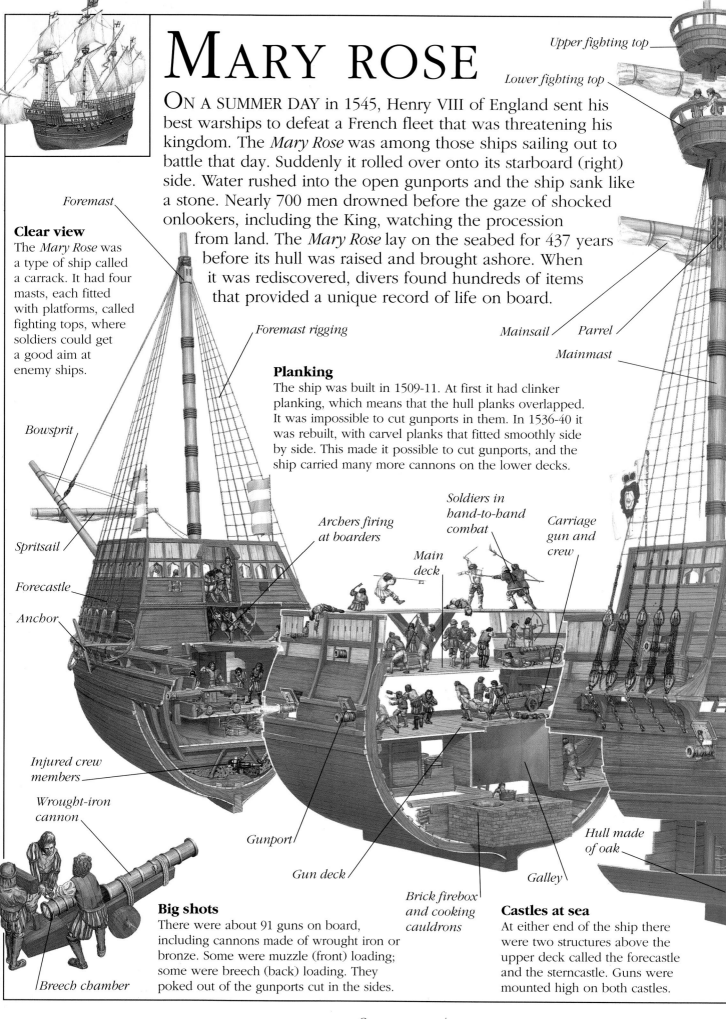

MARY ROSE

ON A SUMMER DAY in 1545, Henry VIII of England sent his best warships to defeat a French fleet that was threatening his kingdom. The *Mary Rose* was among those ships sailing out to battle that day. Suddenly it rolled over onto its starboard (right) side. Water rushed into the open gunports and the ship sank like a stone. Nearly 700 men drowned before the gaze of shocked onlookers, including the King, watching the procession from land. The *Mary Rose* lay on the seabed for 437 years before its hull was raised and brought ashore. When it was rediscovered, divers found hundreds of items that provided a unique record of life on board.

Upper fighting top

Lower fighting top

Foremast

Clear view

The *Mary Rose* was a type of ship called a carrack. It had four masts, each fitted with platforms, called fighting tops, where soldiers could get a good aim at enemy ships.

Foremast rigging

Mainsail **Parrel**

Mainmast

Planking

The ship was built in 1509-11. At first it had clinker planking, which means that the hull planks overlapped. It was impossible to cut gunports in them. In 1536-40 it was rebuilt, with carvel planks that fitted smoothly side by side. This made it possible to cut gunports, and the ship carried many more cannons on the lower decks.

Bowsprit

Spritsail

Forecastle

Anchor

Archers firing at boarders

Soldiers in hand-to-hand combat

Carriage gun and crew

Main deck

Injured crew members

Wrought-iron cannon

Gunport

Gun deck

Brick firebox and cooking cauldrons

Galley

Hull made of oak

Breech chamber

Big shots

There were about 91 guns on board, including cannons made of wrought iron or bronze. Some were muzzle (front) loading; some were breech (back) loading. They poked out of the gunports cut in the sides.

Castles at sea

At either end of the ship there were two structures above the upper deck called the forecastle and the sterncastle. Guns were mounted high on both castles.

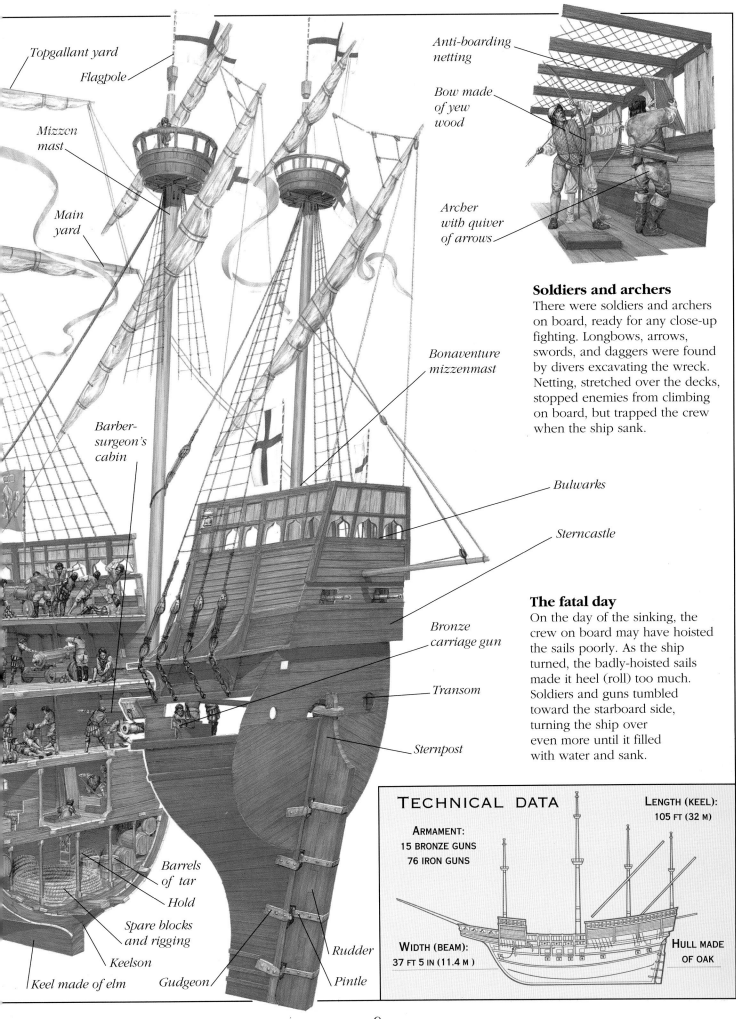

Topgallant yard

Flagpole

Mizzen mast

Main yard

Barber-surgeon's cabin

Anti-boarding netting

Bow made of yew wood

Archer with quiver of arrows

Soldiers and archers

There were soldiers and archers on board, ready for any close-up fighting. Longbows, arrows, swords, and daggers were found by divers excavating the wreck. Netting, stretched over the decks, stopped enemies from climbing on board, but trapped the crew when the ship sank.

Bonaventure mizzenmast

Bulwarks

Sterncastle

The fatal day

On the day of the sinking, the crew on board may have hoisted the sails poorly. As the ship turned, the badly-hoisted sails made it heel (roll) too much. Soldiers and guns tumbled toward the starboard side, turning the ship over even more until it filled with water and sank.

Bronze carriage gun

Transom

Sternpost

Barrels of tar

Hold

Spare blocks and rigging

Keelson

Keel made of elm

Gudgeon

Rudder

Pintle

TECHNICAL DATA

LENGTH (KEEL): 105 FT (32 M)

ARMAMENT:
15 BRONZE GUNS
76 IRON GUNS

WIDTH (BEAM): 37 FT 5 IN (11.4 M)

HULL MADE OF OAK

MAYFLOWER

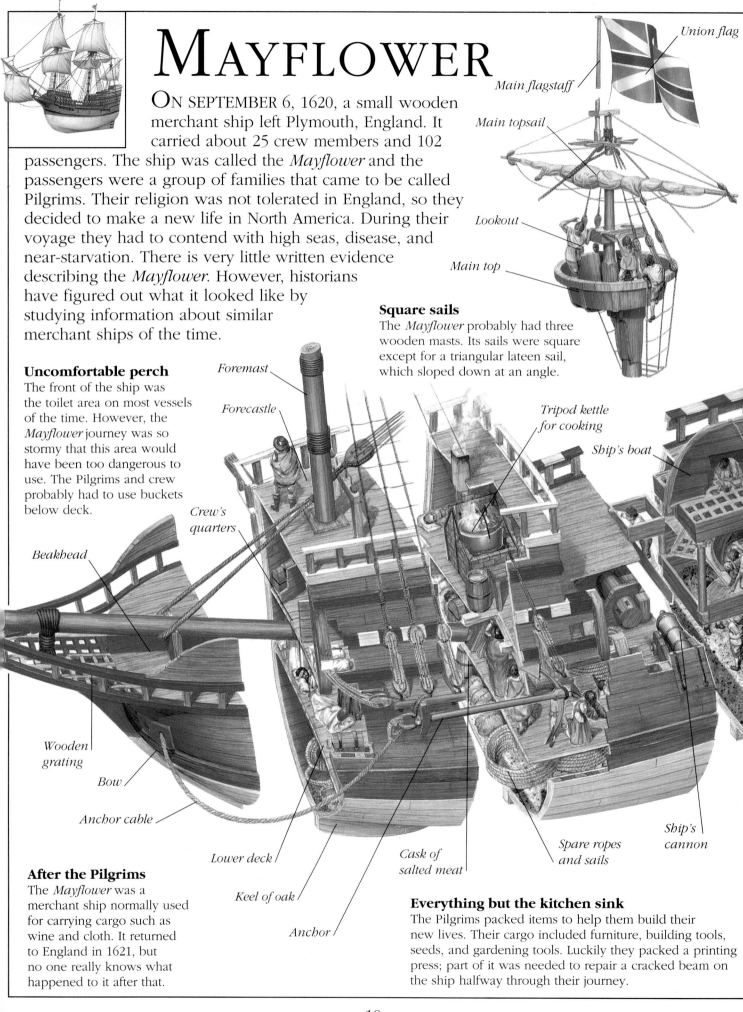

ON SEPTEMBER 6, 1620, a small wooden merchant ship left Plymouth, England. It carried about 25 crew members and 102 passengers. The ship was called the *Mayflower* and the passengers were a group of families that came to be called Pilgrims. Their religion was not tolerated in England, so they decided to make a new life in North America. During their voyage they had to contend with high seas, disease, and near-starvation. There is very little written evidence describing the *Mayflower*. However, historians have figured out what it looked like by studying information about similar merchant ships of the time.

Union flag

Main flagstaff

Main topsail

Lookout

Main top

Square sails
The *Mayflower* probably had three wooden masts. Its sails were square except for a triangular lateen sail, which sloped down at an angle.

Uncomfortable perch
The front of the ship was the toilet area on most vessels of the time. However, the *Mayflower* journey was so stormy that this area would have been too dangerous to use. The Pilgrims and crew probably had to use buckets below deck.

Foremast

Forecastle

Tripod kettle for cooking

Ship's boat

Crew's quarters

Beakhead

Wooden grating

Bow

Anchor cable

Lower deck

Keel of oak

Anchor

Cask of salted meat

Spare ropes and sails

Ship's cannon

After the Pilgrims
The *Mayflower* was a merchant ship normally used for carrying cargo such as wine and cloth. It returned to England in 1621, but no one really knows what happened to it after that.

Everything but the kitchen sink
The Pilgrims packed items to help them build their new lives. Their cargo included furniture, building tools, seeds, and gardening tools. Luckily they packed a printing press; part of it was needed to repair a cracked beam on the ship halfway through their journey.

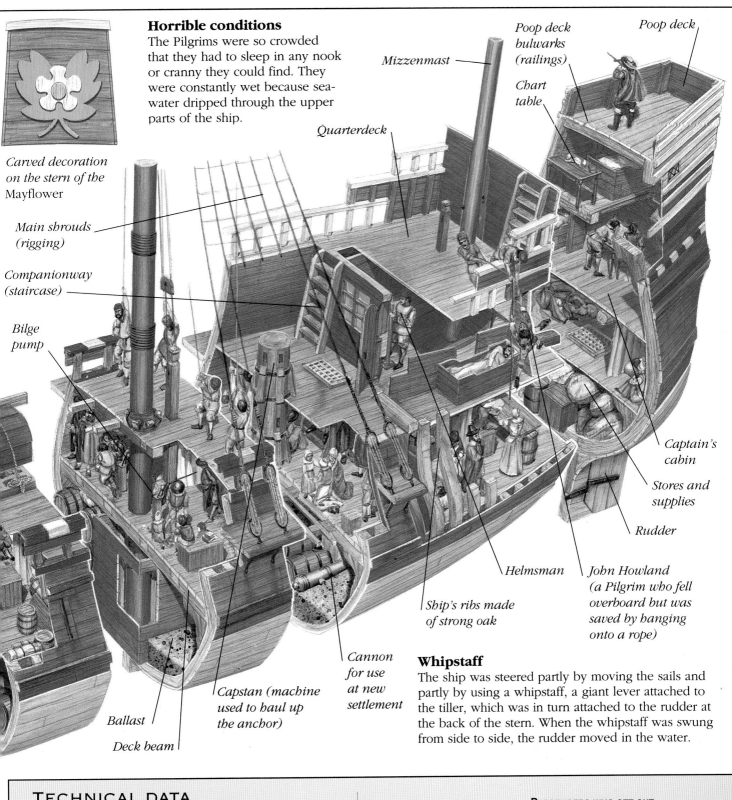

Horrible conditions

The Pilgrims were so crowded that they had to sleep in any nook or cranny they could find. They were constantly wet because sea-water dripped through the upper parts of the ship.

Poop deck bulwarks (railings)

Poop deck

Mizzenmast

Chart table

Quarterdeck

Carved decoration on the stern of the Mayflower

Main shrouds (rigging)

Companionway (staircase)

Bilge pump

Captain's cabin

Stores and supplies

Rudder

Helmsman

John Howland (a Pilgrim who fell overboard but was saved by hanging onto a rope)

Ship's ribs made of strong oak

Cannon for use at new settlement

Capstan (machine used to haul up the anchor)

Ballast

Deck beam

Whipstaff

The ship was steered partly by moving the sails and partly by using a whipstaff, a giant lever attached to the tiller, which was in turn attached to the rudder at the back of the stern. When the whipstaff was swung from side to side, the rudder moved in the water.

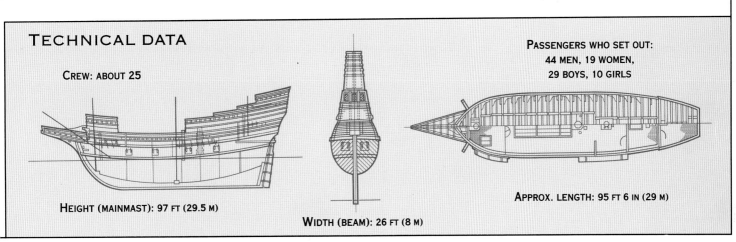

TECHNICAL DATA

CREW: ABOUT 25

PASSENGERS WHO SET OUT:
44 MEN, 19 WOMEN,
29 BOYS, 10 GIRLS

HEIGHT (MAINMAST): 97 FT (29.5 M)

WIDTH (BEAM): 26 FT (8 M)

APPROX. LENGTH: 95 FT 6 IN (29 M)

11

HMS PANDORA

IN 1790, THE HMS *PANDORA* set sail from England to catch the most notorious mutineers in naval history. Its story began with the voyage of another ship, the HMS *Bounty*. In 1787, the *Bounty* sailed to Tahiti. The exotic island seemed like paradise to the *Bounty's* disgruntled crewmen, and they mutinied to avoid returning home. The *Pandora* succeeded in capturing fourteen mutineers, but then hit the Great Barrier Reef off North Queensland, Australia, and sank. In 1977, the wreck was found, and its contents have since been carefully excavated.

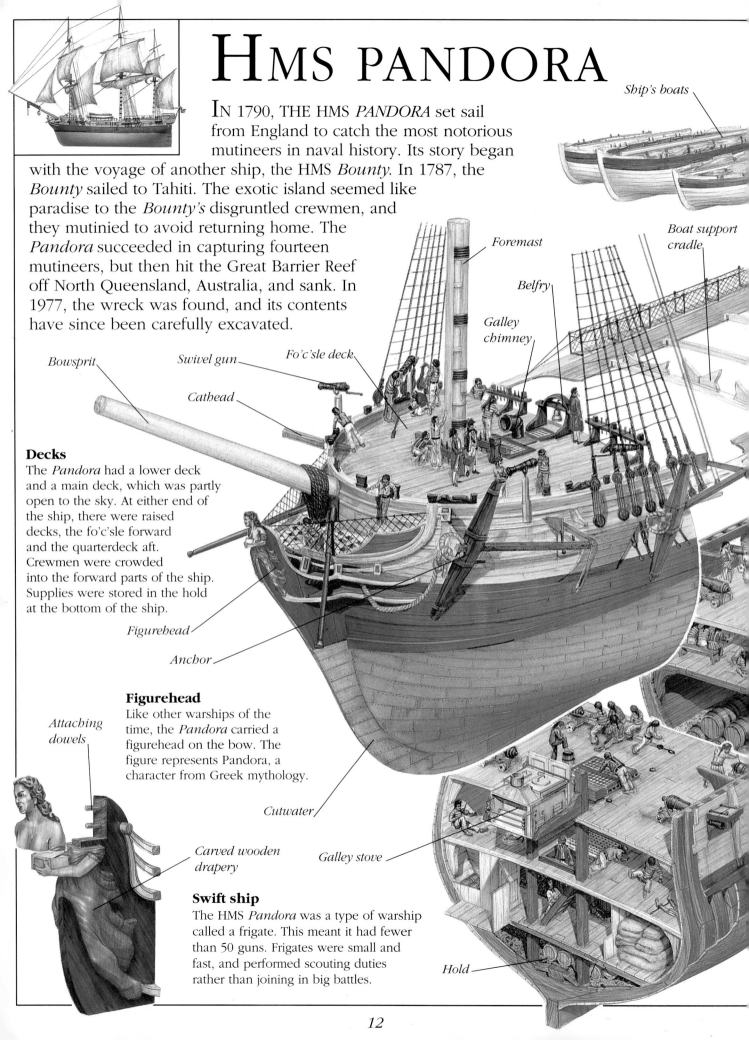

Ship's boats

Foremast

Boat support cradle

Belfry

Galley chimney

Bowsprit

Swivel gun

Fo'c'sle deck

Cathead

Decks
The *Pandora* had a lower deck and a main deck, which was partly open to the sky. At either end of the ship, there were raised decks, the fo'c'sle forward and the quarterdeck aft. Crewmen were crowded into the forward parts of the ship. Supplies were stored in the hold at the bottom of the ship.

Figurehead

Anchor

Figurehead
Like other warships of the time, the *Pandora* carried a figurehead on the bow. The figure represents Pandora, a character from Greek mythology.

Attaching dowels

Cutwater

Carved wooden drapery

Galley stove

Swift ship
The HMS *Pandora* was a type of warship called a frigate. This meant it had fewer than 50 guns. Frigates were small and fast, and performed scouting duties rather than joining in big battles.

Hold

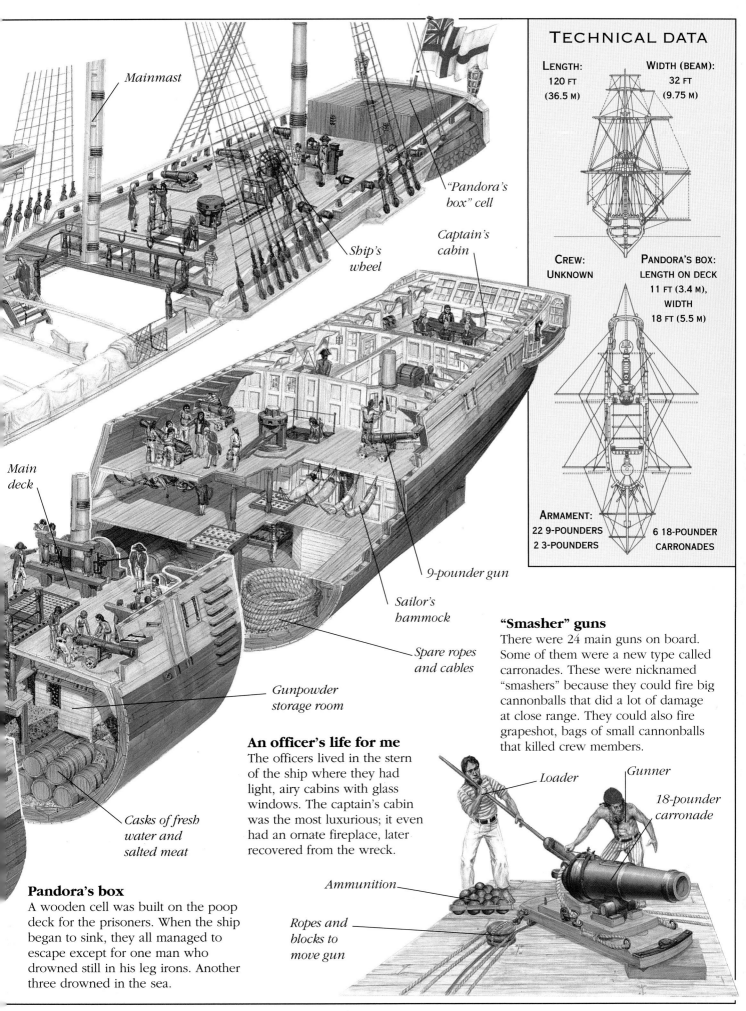

Mainmast

"Pandora's box" cell

Captain's cabin

Ship's wheel

Main deck

9-pounder gun

Sailor's hammock

Spare ropes and cables

Gunpowder storage room

Casks of fresh water and salted meat

"Smasher" guns

There were 24 main guns on board. Some of them were a new type called carronades. These were nicknamed "smashers" because they could fire big cannonballs that did a lot of damage at close range. They could also fire grapeshot, bags of small cannonballs that killed crew members.

An officer's life for me

The officers lived in the stern of the ship where they had light, airy cabins with glass windows. The captain's cabin was the most luxurious; it even had an ornate fireplace, later recovered from the wreck.

Loader

Gunner

18-pounder carronade

Ammunition

Ropes and blocks to move gun

Pandora's box

A wooden cell was built on the poop deck for the prisoners. When the ship began to sink, they all managed to escape except for one man who drowned still in his leg irons. Another three drowned in the sea.

BATTLESHIP

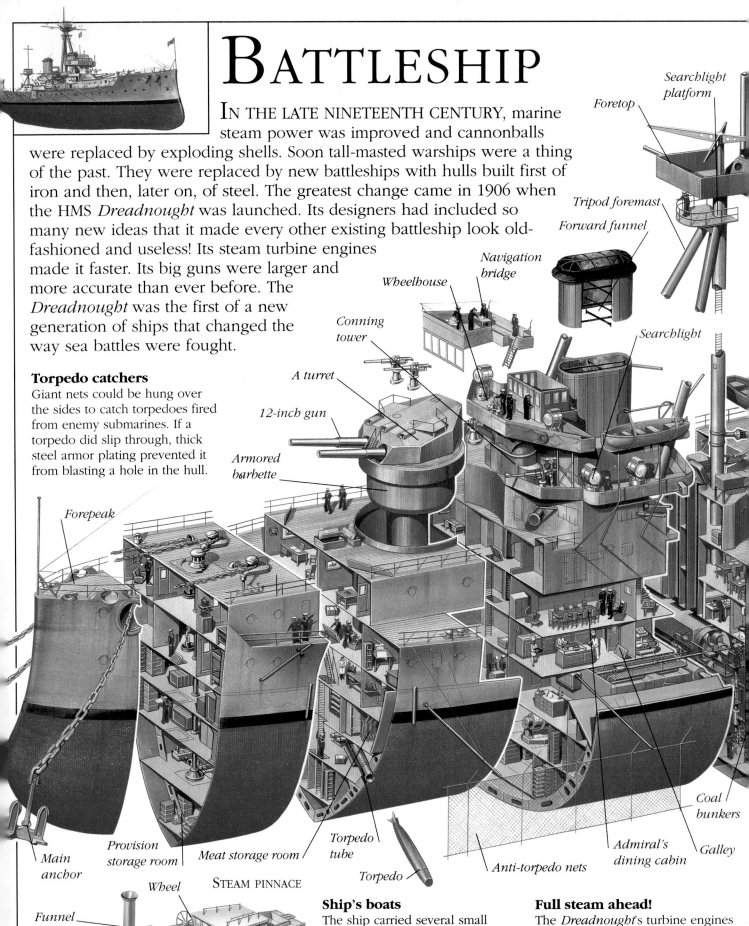

IN THE LATE NINETEENTH CENTURY, marine steam power was improved and cannonballs were replaced by exploding shells. Soon tall-masted warships were a thing of the past. They were replaced by new battleships with hulls built first of iron and then, later on, of steel. The greatest change came in 1906 when the HMS *Dreadnought* was launched. Its designers had included so many new ideas that it made every other existing battleship look old-fashioned and useless! Its steam turbine engines made it faster. Its big guns were larger and more accurate than ever before. The *Dreadnought* was the first of a new generation of ships that changed the way sea battles were fought.

Torpedo catchers

Giant nets could be hung over the sides to catch torpedoes fired from enemy submarines. If a torpedo did slip through, thick steel armor plating prevented it from blasting a hole in the hull.

Searchlight platform

Foretop

Tripod foremast

Forward funnel

Navigation bridge

Wheelhouse

Conning tower

A turret

12-inch gun

Armored barbette

Searchlight

Forepeak

Main anchor

Provision storage room

Meat storage room

Torpedo tube

Torpedo

Anti-torpedo nets

Coal bunkers

Admiral's dining cabin

Galley

Wheel

STEAM PINNACE

Funnel

Cabin

Ship's boats

The ship carried several small boats like the steam-powered pinnace shown here. They were used to ferry officers and supplies to and from shore.

Full steam ahead!

The *Dreadnought*'s turbine engines were fast and reliable. Inside them, steam pushed against thousands of blades mounted on shafts that spun around, driving the ship's propellers.

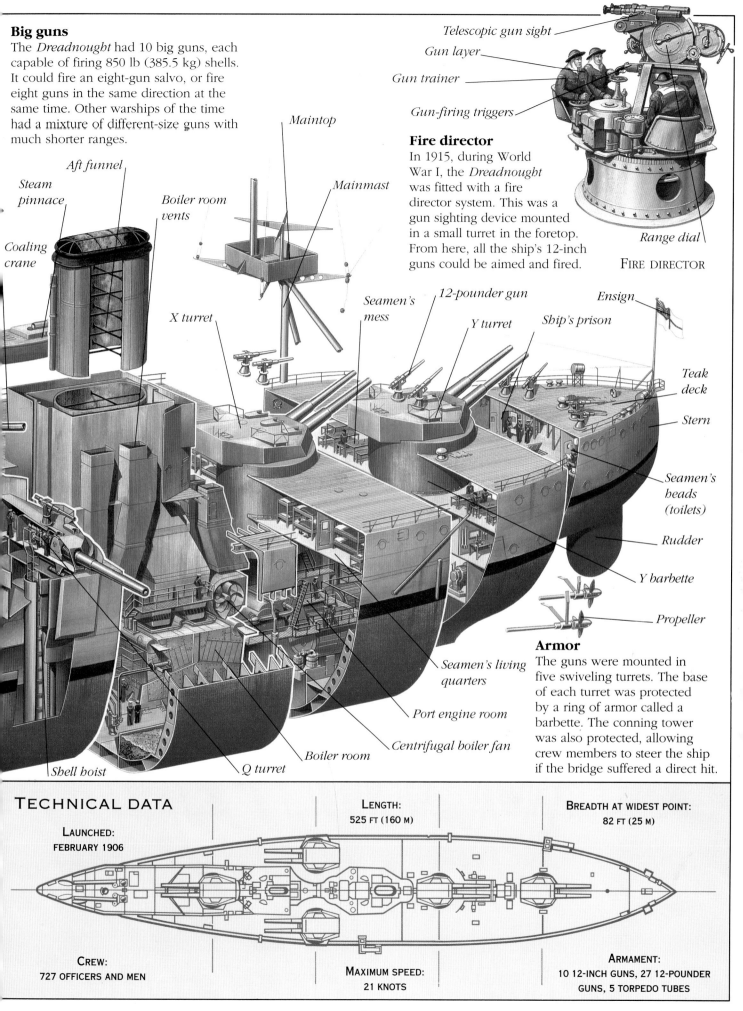

Big guns

The *Dreadnought* had 10 big guns, each capable of firing 850 lb (385.5 kg) shells. It could fire an eight-gun salvo, or fire eight guns in the same direction at the same time. Other warships of the time had a mixture of different-size guns with much shorter ranges.

Telescopic gun sight

Gun layer

Gun trainer

Gun-firing triggers

Fire director

In 1915, during World War I, the *Dreadnought* was fitted with a fire director system. This was a gun sighting device mounted in a small turret in the foretop. From here, all the ship's 12-inch guns could be aimed and fired.

Range dial

FIRE DIRECTOR

Maintop

Mainmast

Aft funnel

Steam pinnace

Boiler room vents

Coaling crane

X turret

Seamen's mess

12-pounder gun

Y turret

Ship's prison

Ensign

Teak deck

Stern

Seamen's heads (toilets)

Rudder

Y barbette

Propeller

Armor

The guns were mounted in five swiveling turrets. The base of each turret was protected by a ring of armor called a barbette. The conning tower was also protected, allowing crew members to steer the ship if the bridge suffered a direct hit.

Seamen's living quarters

Port engine room

Centrifugal boiler fan

Shell hoist

Q turret

Boiler room

TECHNICAL DATA

LENGTH:
525 FT (160 M)

BREADTH AT WIDEST POINT:
82 FT (25 M)

LAUNCHED:
FEBRUARY 1906

CREW:
727 OFFICERS AND MEN

MAXIMUM SPEED:
21 KNOTS

ARMAMENT:
10 12-INCH GUNS, 27 12-POUNDER
GUNS, 5 TORPEDO TUBES

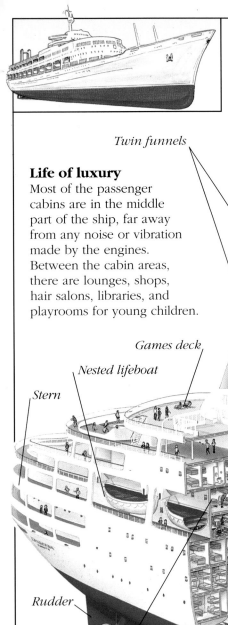

CANBERRA

A MODERN OCEAN LINER is more than just a sailing ship. It is a huge floating hotel with lots of luxuries on board. The passengers can sunbathe on deck, jump in a swimming pool, play sports, go shopping, or watch a movie. The most important job for the crew is to make sure that everyone has a comfortable and relaxing trip. This picture shows the *Canberra*, launched in 1960.

When the *Canberra* was built, it was hailed as the shape of things to come, and, indeed, it is still in service today. Its sleek, elegant hull and below-deck layout have also been copied on ocean liners all over the world.

Life of luxury
Most of the passenger cabins are in the middle part of the ship, far away from any noise or vibration made by the engines. Between the cabin areas, there are lounges, shops, hair salons, libraries, and playrooms for young children.

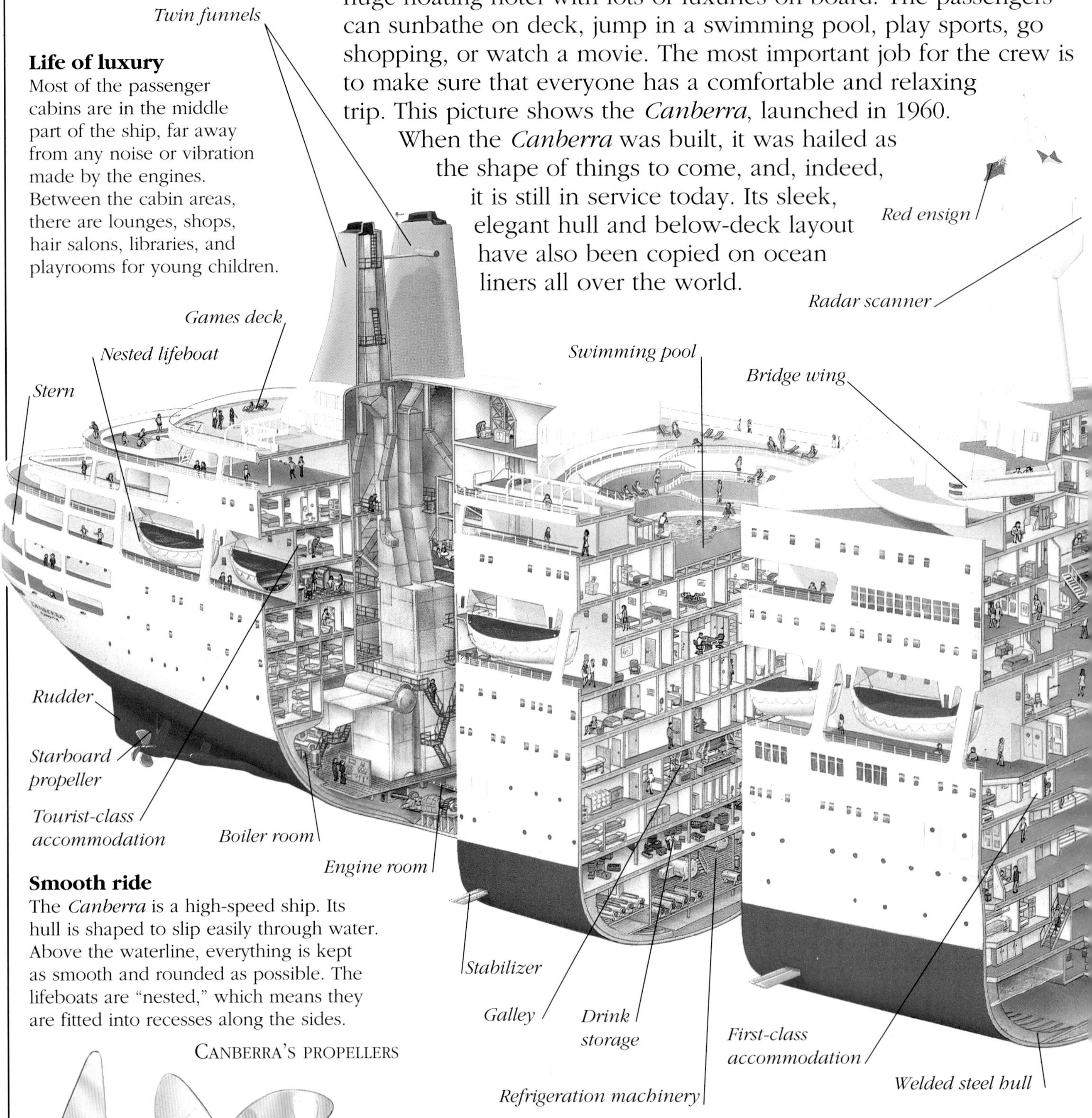

Twin funnels

Games deck

Nested lifeboat

Stern

Rudder

Starboard propeller

Tourist-class accommodation

Boiler room

Engine room

Swimming pool

Bridge wing

Red ensign

Radar scanner

Stabilizer

Galley

Drink storage

Refrigeration machinery

First-class accommodation

Welded steel hull

Smooth ride
The *Canberra* is a high-speed ship. Its hull is shaped to slip easily through water. Above the waterline, everything is kept as smooth and rounded as possible. The lifeboats are "nested," which means they are fitted into recesses along the sides.

CANBERRA'S PROPELLERS

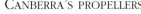

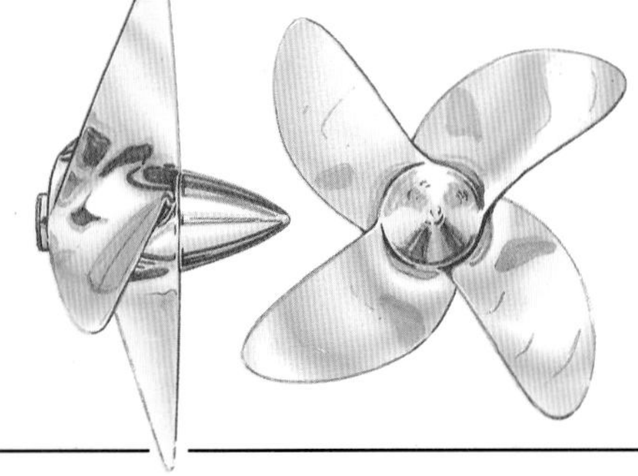

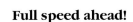

Full speed ahead!
Two propellers are situated at the stern of the ship, on either side of the hull. They push the *Canberra* forward through the water at an average speed of 27.5 knots.

Powerful engines
Unlike most previous liners, the *Canberra's* engines are near the stern. Steam-driven turbines create electricity to run motors, which turn the two propellers underneath the stern. The ship uses 1 gallon (4.5 liters) of fuel to move forward 53 ft (16 m).

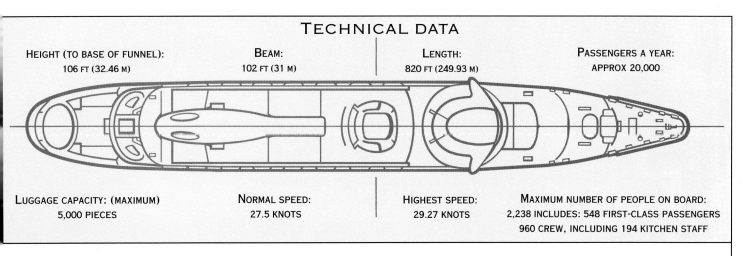

HEIGHT (TO BASE OF FUNNEL): 106 FT (32.46 M)	**BEAM:** 102 FT (31 M)	**LENGTH:** 820 FT (249.93 M)	**PASSENGERS A YEAR:** APPROX 20,000

LUGGAGE CAPACITY: (MAXIMUM) 5,000 PIECES	**NORMAL SPEED:** 27.5 KNOTS	**HIGHEST SPEED:** 29.27 KNOTS	**MAXIMUM NUMBER OF PEOPLE ON BOARD:** 2,238 INCLUDES: 548 FIRST-CLASS PASSENGERS 960 CREW, INCLUDING 194 KITCHEN STAFF

Captain's command post

The top part of the ship rises above the main decks. It is called the superstructure, and it houses the bridge, where the captain works. There are also officers' cabins, and a navigation room with radar and satellite-tracking equipment.

Canberra crew

There is a crew of 960 people. This includes waiters, cooks, cleaners, entertainers, and lots of other hotel-type staff as well as the seamen who make sure that the journey goes smoothly.

Food facts

It takes 90 days for the *Canberra* to complete a world cruise. During this time, 675,000 main meals are prepared using, among other ingredients, 400,000 eggs. More than 250,000 cakes and pastries are baked, together with 35,000 loaves and half a million bread rolls!

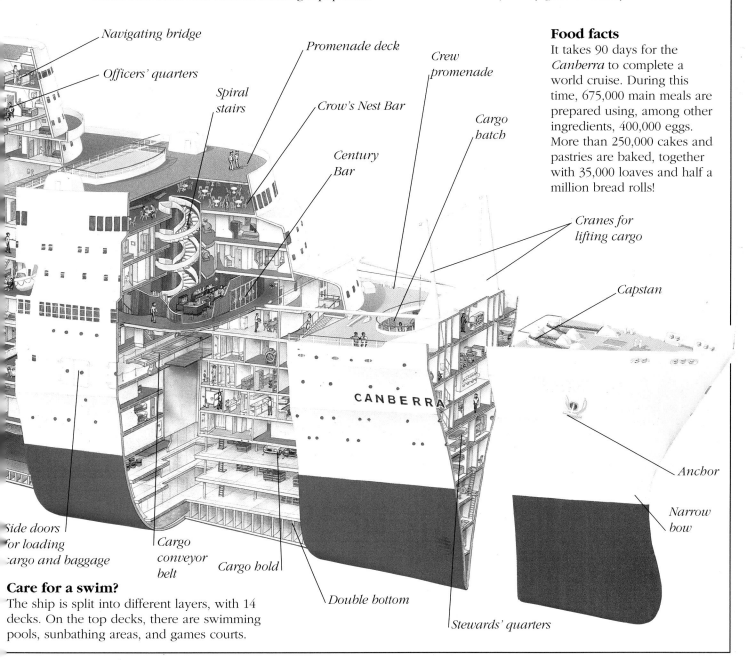

Elevator

Navigating bridge

Officers' quarters

Spiral stairs

Promenade deck

Crow's Nest Bar

Century Bar

Crew promenade

Cargo hatch

Cranes for lifting cargo

Capstan

CANBERRA

Anchor

Narrow bow

Side doors for loading cargo and baggage

Cargo conveyor belt

Cargo hold

Double bottom

Stewards' quarters

Care for a swim?

The ship is split into different layers, with 14 decks. On the top decks, there are swimming pools, sunbathing areas, and games courts.

AIRCRAFT CARRIER

AIRCRAFT CARRIERS ARE THE WORLD'S biggest warships. Their giant steel hulls tower high above the waves and their flight decks stretch out for more than the length of two football fields. A carrier does not need to get close to an enemy; its aircraft can take off from the deck to bomb a target far away. During World War II, American Essex-class aircraft carriers fought important battles in the Pacific Ocean. Many of their features are still on today's carriers. Essex-class ships carried over a hundred airplanes, thousands of crew members, and big stores of ammunition and fuel. This picture shows the USS *Lexington*, a carrier that served in the Pacific.

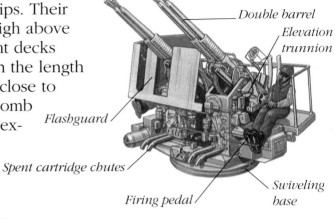

BOFORS 40-MM AA GUNS

Double barrel

Elevation trunnion

Flashguard

Spent cartridge chutes

Firing pedal

Swiveling base

Shooting down the enemy
Carriers could be attacked by enemy airplanes, so they were fitted with lots of small rapid-firing anti-aircraft ("AA") guns that worked at close range. Crew members wore white hoods to protect themselves from flash burns when they fired.

Kamikaze!
One of the main dangers to World War II carriers came from Japanese *Kamikaze* suicide planes. These planes were piloted bombs, packed with explosives, that would blow up when they crashed into enemy ships.

Up and away
For an aircraft to take off from the ship, it needed to build up speed quickly. It was attached by a hook to runners that slid along tracks on the flight deck. Powered by steam, the runners would shoot the airplane forward, the hook would uncouple, and the aircraft took off. This equipment was called a steam catapult.

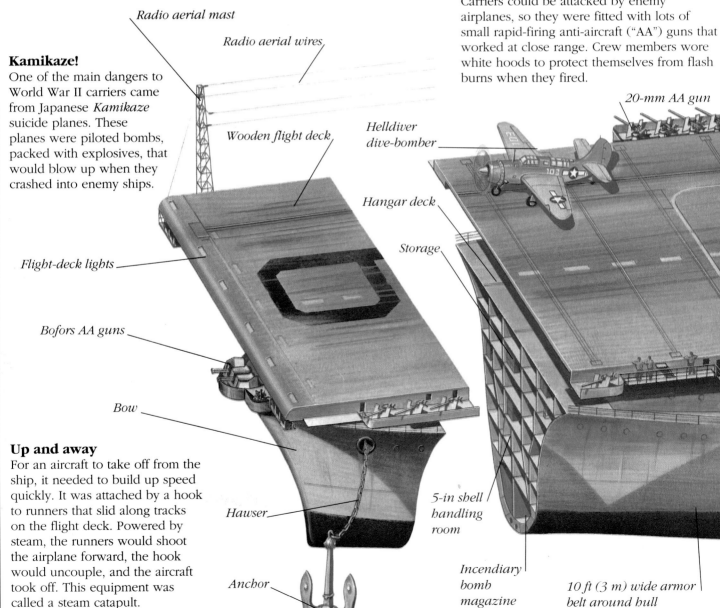

Radio aerial mast

Radio aerial wires

Wooden flight deck

Helldiver dive-bomber

20-mm AA gun

Hangar deck

Storage

Flight-deck lights

Bofors AA guns

Bow

Hawser

Anchor

5-in shell handling room

Incendiary bomb magazine

10 ft (3 m) wide armor belt around hull

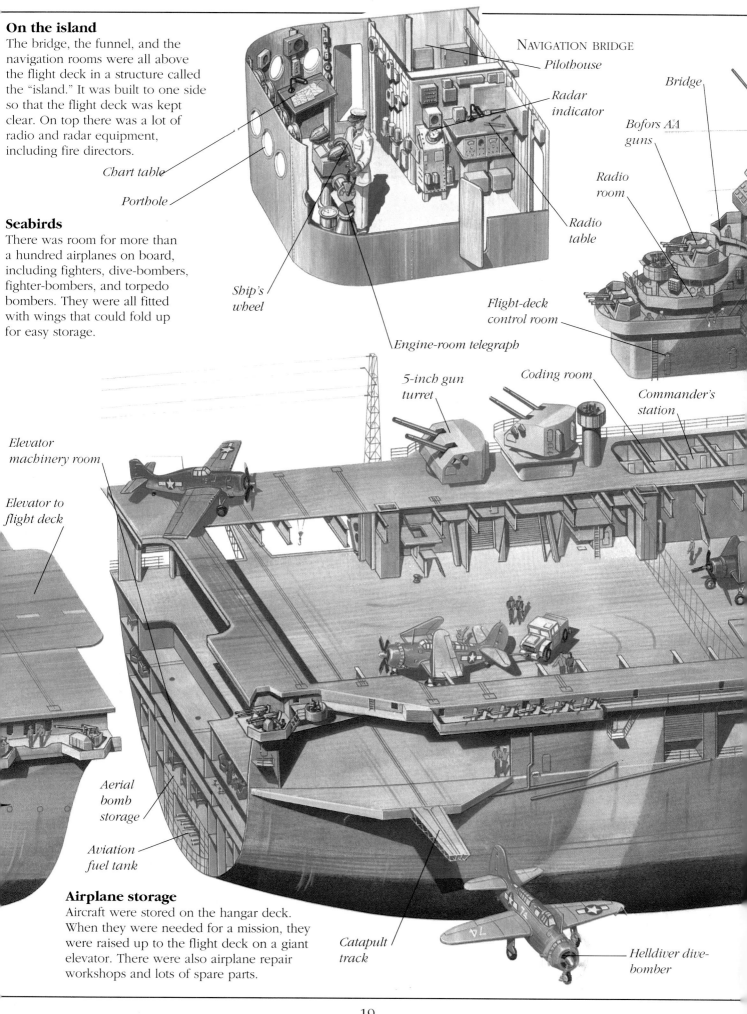

On the island

The bridge, the funnel, and the navigation rooms were all above the flight deck in a structure called the "island." It was built to one side so that the flight deck was kept clear. On top there was a lot of radio and radar equipment, including fire directors.

Seabirds

There was room for more than a hundred airplanes on board, including fighters, dive-bombers, fighter-bombers, and torpedo bombers. They were all fitted with wings that could fold up for easy storage.

Airplane storage

Aircraft were stored on the hangar deck. When they were needed for a mission, they were raised up to the flight deck on a giant elevator. There were also airplane repair workshops and lots of spare parts.

NAVIGATION BRIDGE

Pilothouse

Bridge

Radar indicator

Bofors AA guns

Radio room

Chart table

Porthole

Radio table

Ship's wheel

Flight-deck control room

Coding room

Engine-room telegraph

Commander's station

5-inch gun turret

Elevator machinery room

Elevator to flight deck

Aerial bomb storage

Aviation fuel tank

Catapult track

Helldiver dive-bomber

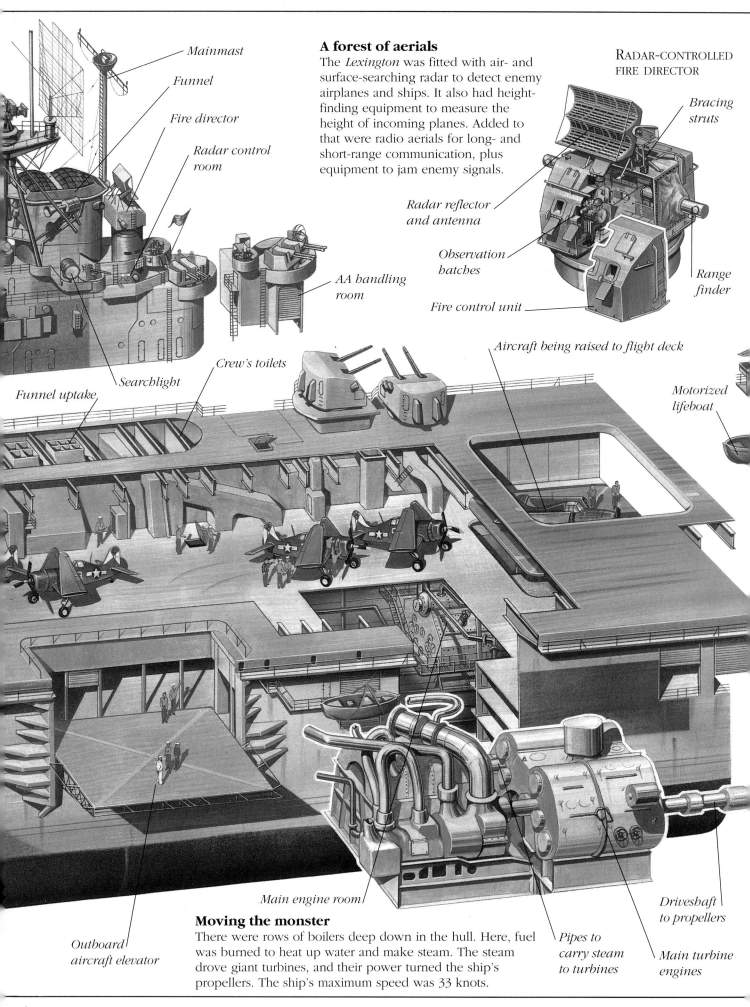

Mainmast

Funnel

Fire director

Radar control room

A forest of aerials

The *Lexington* was fitted with air- and surface-searching radar to detect enemy airplanes and ships. It also had height-finding equipment to measure the height of incoming planes. Added to that were radio aerials for long- and short-range communication, plus equipment to jam enemy signals.

RADAR-CONTROLLED FIRE DIRECTOR

Bracing struts

Radar reflector and antenna

Observation hatches

Range finder

Fire control unit

AA handling room

Aircraft being raised to flight deck

Motorized lifeboat

Searchlight

Crew's toilets

Funnel uptake

Outboard aircraft elevator

Main engine room

Pipes to carry steam to turbines

Driveshaft to propellers

Main turbine engines

Moving the monster

There were rows of boilers deep down in the hull. Here, fuel was burned to heat up water and make steam. The steam drove giant turbines, and their power turned the ship's propellers. The ship's maximum speed was 33 knots.

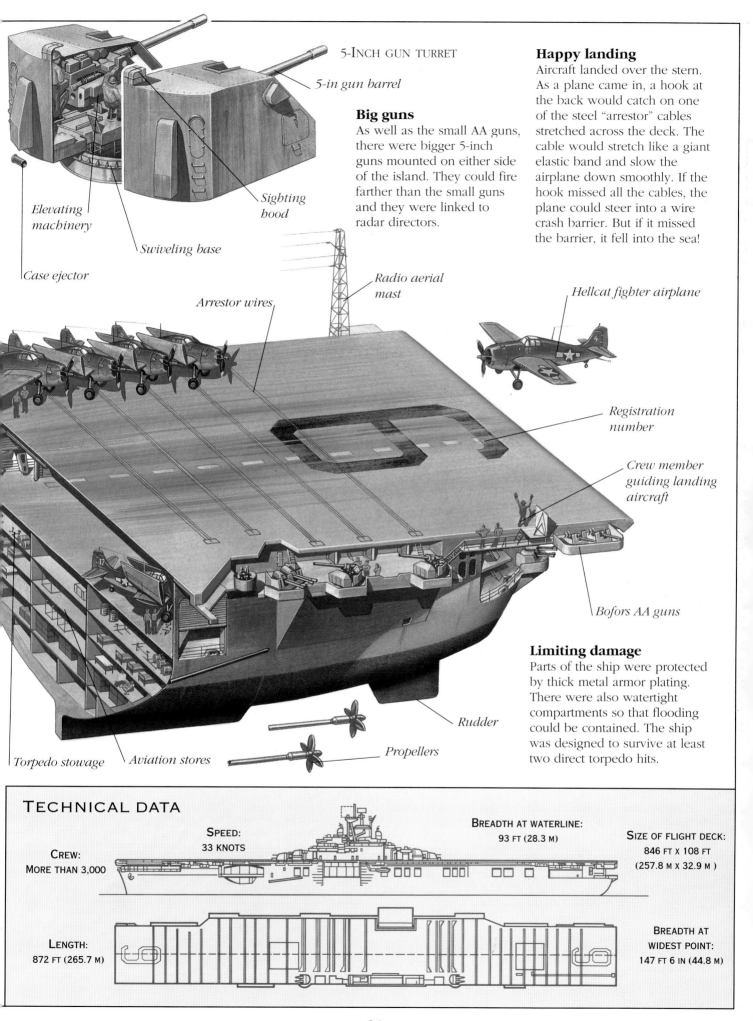

5-INCH GUN TURRET

5-in gun barrel

Sighting hood

Elevating machinery

Swiveling base

Case ejector

Big guns
As well as the small AA guns, there were bigger 5-inch guns mounted on either side of the island. They could fire farther than the small guns and they were linked to radar directors.

Happy landing
Aircraft landed over the stern. As a plane came in, a hook at the back would catch on one of the steel "arrestor" cables stretched across the deck. The cable would stretch like a giant elastic band and slow the airplane down smoothly. If the hook missed all the cables, the plane could steer into a wire crash barrier. But if it missed the barrier, it fell into the sea!

Radio aerial mast

Arrestor wires

Hellcat fighter airplane

Registration number

Crew member guiding landing aircraft

Bofors AA guns

Limiting damage
Parts of the ship were protected by thick metal armor plating. There were also watertight compartments so that flooding could be contained. The ship was designed to survive at least two direct torpedo hits.

Rudder

Propellers

Torpedo stowage   *Aviation stores*

TECHNICAL DATA

CREW:
MORE THAN 3,000

SPEED:
33 KNOTS

BREADTH AT WATERLINE:
93 FT (28.3 M)

SIZE OF FLIGHT DECK:
846 FT X 108 FT
(257.8 M X 32.9 M)

LENGTH:
872 FT (265.7 M)

BREADTH AT WIDEST POINT:
147 FT 6 IN (44.8 M)

CHINESE JUNK

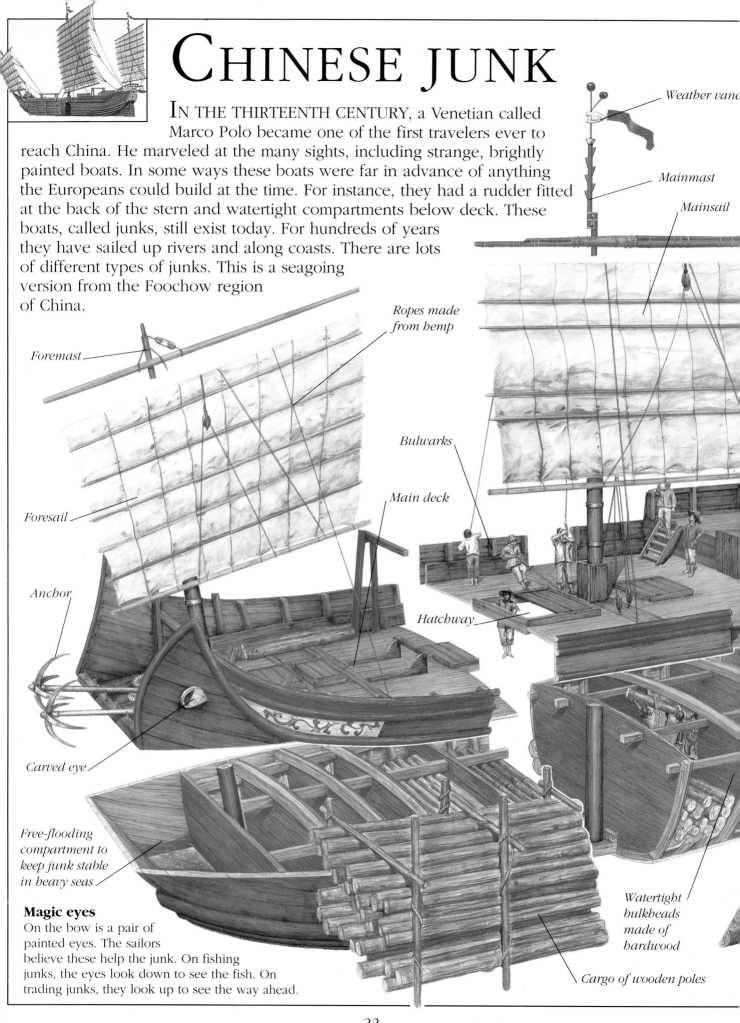

IN THE THIRTEENTH CENTURY, a Venetian called
Marco Polo became one of the first travelers ever to
reach China. He marveled at the many sights, including strange, brightly
painted boats. In some ways these boats were far in advance of anything
the Europeans could build at the time. For instance, they had a rudder fitted
at the back of the stern and watertight compartments below deck. These
boats, called junks, still exist today. For hundreds of years
they have sailed up rivers and along coasts. There are lots
of different types of junks. This is a seagoing
version from the Foochow region
of China.

Weather vane

Mainmast

Mainsail

Ropes made from hemp

Foremast

Bulwarks

Main deck

Foresail

Anchor

Hatchway

Carved eye

Free-flooding compartment to keep junk stable in heavy seas

Watertight bulkheads made of hardwood

Magic eyes
On the bow is a pair of
painted eyes. The sailors
believe these help the junk. On fishing
junks, the eyes look down to see the fish. On
trading junks, they look up to see the way ahead.

Cargo of wooden poles

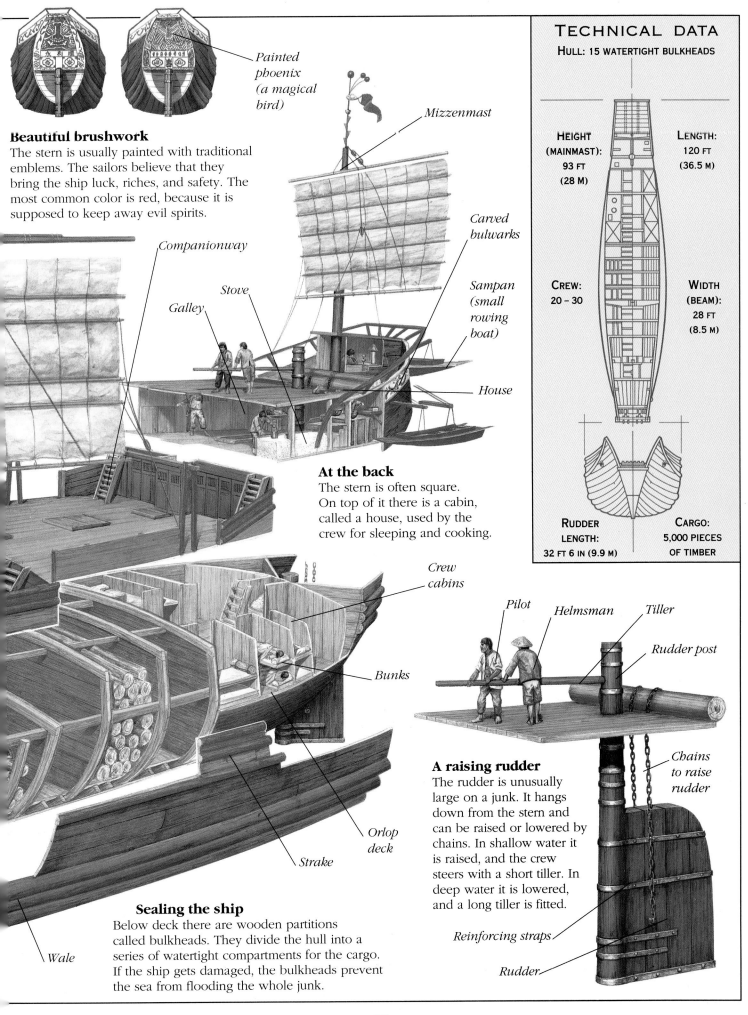

Painted
*phoenix
(a magical
bird)*

Mizzenmast

Beautiful brushwork

The stern is usually painted with traditional emblems. The sailors believe that they bring the ship luck, riches, and safety. The most common color is red, because it is supposed to keep away evil spirits.

Companionway

Stove

Galley

*Carved
bulwarks*

*Sampan
(small
rowing
boat)*

House

At the back

The stern is often square. On top of it there is a cabin, called a house, used by the crew for sleeping and cooking.

*Crew
cabins*

Bunks

*Orlop
deck*

Strake

Wale

Sealing the ship

Below deck there are wooden partitions called bulkheads. They divide the hull into a series of watertight compartments for the cargo. If the ship gets damaged, the bulkheads prevent the sea from flooding the whole junk.

TECHNICAL DATA

HULL: 15 WATERTIGHT BULKHEADS

HEIGHT (MAINMAST): 93 FT (28 M)	**LENGTH:** 120 FT (36.5 M)
CREW: 20 – 30	**WIDTH** (BEAM): 28 FT (8.5 M)
RUDDER LENGTH: 32 FT 6 IN (9.9 M)	**CARGO:** 5,000 PIECES OF TIMBER

Pilot

Helmsman

Tiller

Rudder post

*Chains
to raise
rudder*

A raising rudder

The rudder is unusually large on a junk. It hangs down from the stern and can be raised or lowered by chains. In shallow water it is raised, and the crew steers with a short tiller. In deep water it is lowered, and a long tiller is fitted.

Reinforcing straps

Rudder

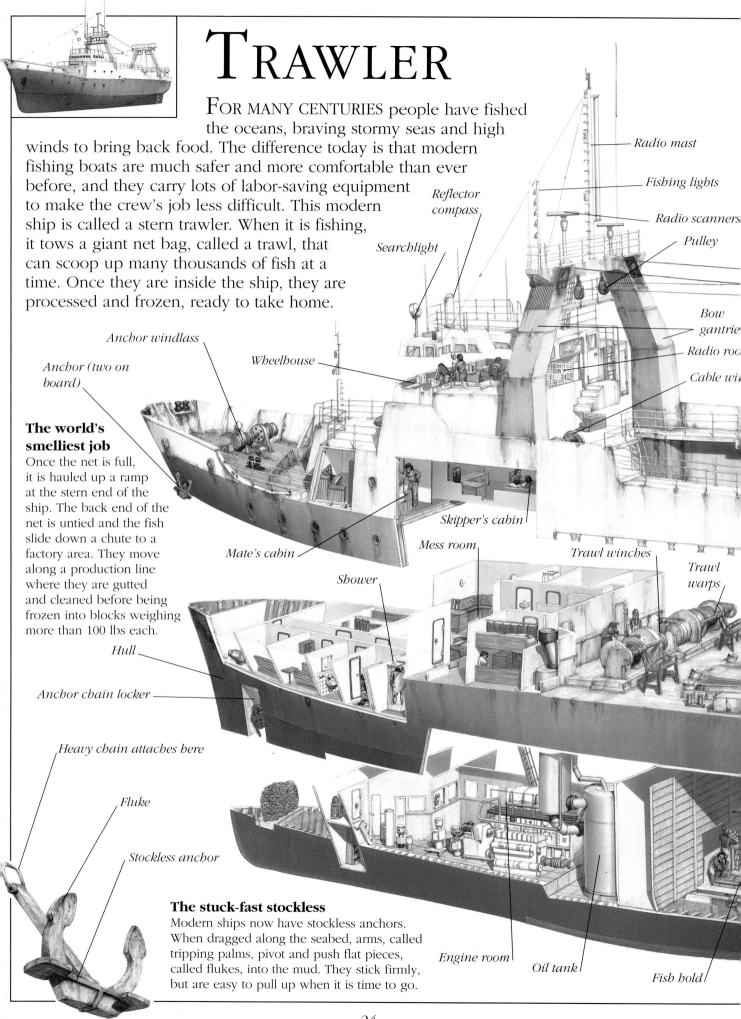

TRAWLER

FOR MANY CENTURIES people have fished the oceans, braving stormy seas and high winds to bring back food. The difference today is that modern fishing boats are much safer and more comfortable than ever before, and they carry lots of labor-saving equipment to make the crew's job less difficult. This modern ship is called a stern trawler. When it is fishing, it tows a giant net bag, called a trawl, that can scoop up many thousands of fish at a time. Once they are inside the ship, they are processed and frozen, ready to take home.

Radio mast

Fishing lights

Radio scanners

Pulley

Reflector compass

Bow gantrie

Searchlight

Radio roc

Cable wi

Anchor windlass

Wheelhouse

Anchor (two on board)

The world's smelliest job

Once the net is full, it is hauled up a ramp at the stern end of the ship. The back end of the net is untied and the fish slide down a chute to a factory area. They move along a production line where they are gutted and cleaned before being frozen into blocks weighing more than 100 lbs each.

Skipper's cabin

Mess room

Trawl winches

Trawl warps

Shower

Mate's cabin

Hull

Anchor chain locker

Heavy chain attaches here

Fluke

Stockless anchor

The stuck-fast stockless

Modern ships now have stockless anchors. When dragged along the seabed, arms, called tripping palms, pivot and push flat pieces, called flukes, into the mud. They stick firmly, but are easy to pull up when it is time to go.

Engine room

Oil tank

Fish hold

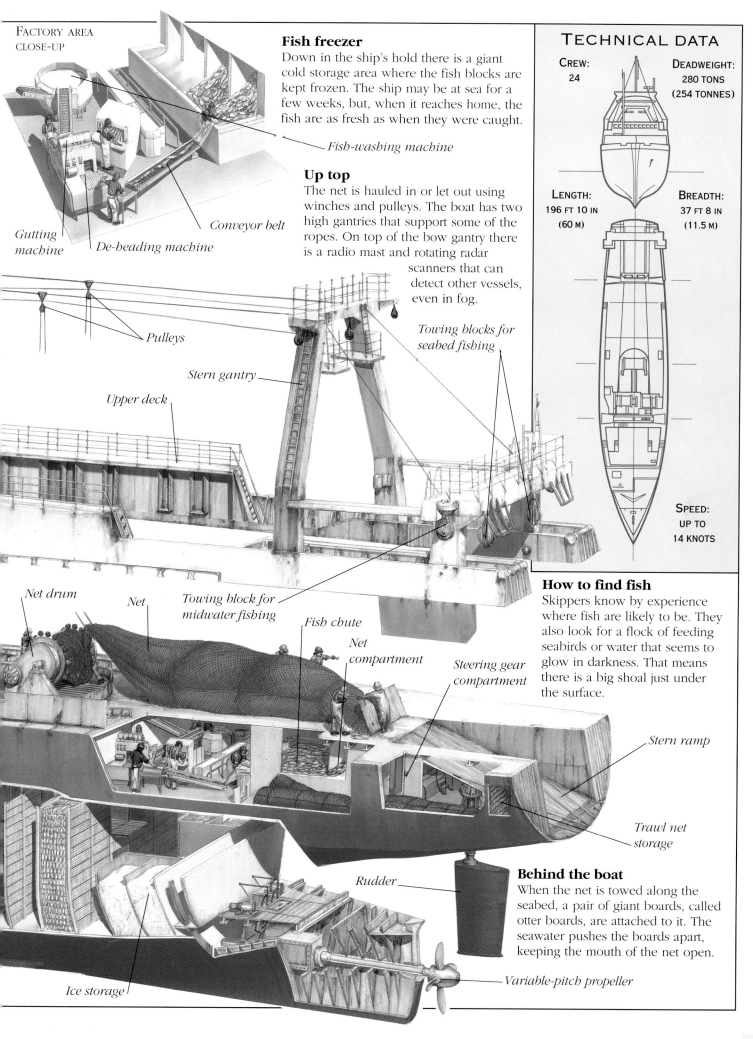

FACTORY AREA CLOSE-UP

Gutting machine

De-heading machine

Conveyor belt

Fish freezer
Down in the ship's hold there is a giant cold storage area where the fish blocks are kept frozen. The ship may be at sea for a few weeks, but, when it reaches home, the fish are as fresh as when they were caught.

Fish-washing machine

Up top
The net is hauled in or let out using winches and pulleys. The boat has two high gantries that support some of the ropes. On top of the bow gantry there is a radio mast and rotating radar scanners that can detect other vessels, even in fog.

Towing blocks for seabed fishing

Pulleys

Stern gantry

Upper deck

TECHNICAL DATA

CREW:
24

DEADWEIGHT:
280 TONS
(254 TONNES)

LENGTH:
196 FT 10 IN
(60 M)

BREADTH:
37 FT 8 IN
(11.5 M)

SPEED:
UP TO
14 KNOTS

Net drum

Net

Towing block for midwater fishing

Fish chute

Net compartment

Steering gear compartment

How to find fish
Skippers know by experience where fish are likely to be. They also look for a flock of feeding seabirds or water that seems to glow in darkness. That means there is a big shoal just under the surface.

Stern ramp

Trawl net storage

Rudder

Behind the boat
When the net is towed along the seabed, a pair of giant boards, called otter boards, are attached to it. The seawater pushes the boards apart, keeping the mouth of the net open.

Ice storage

Variable-pitch propeller

LIFEBOAT

NEXT TIME YOU WATCH A STORM from your window, imagine what it would be like to be at sea off a rugged rocky coast, with wind whipping the waves and rain lashing your face. That's just the kind of weather when boats usually get into trouble. In Britain, a Royal National Lifeboat Institution (RNLI) lifeboat would be called out to rescue the crew. The RNLI is the world's oldest lifeboat service, with stations all around the British coast. The lifeboat shown here is an RNLI Tyne Class. Crew members are all volunteers. Once the lifeboat is called out, the volunteers get to the lifeboat station as fast as they can. As soon as they are on board, the boat runs down a slipway, hits the water with a mighty splash, and races off to the rescue.

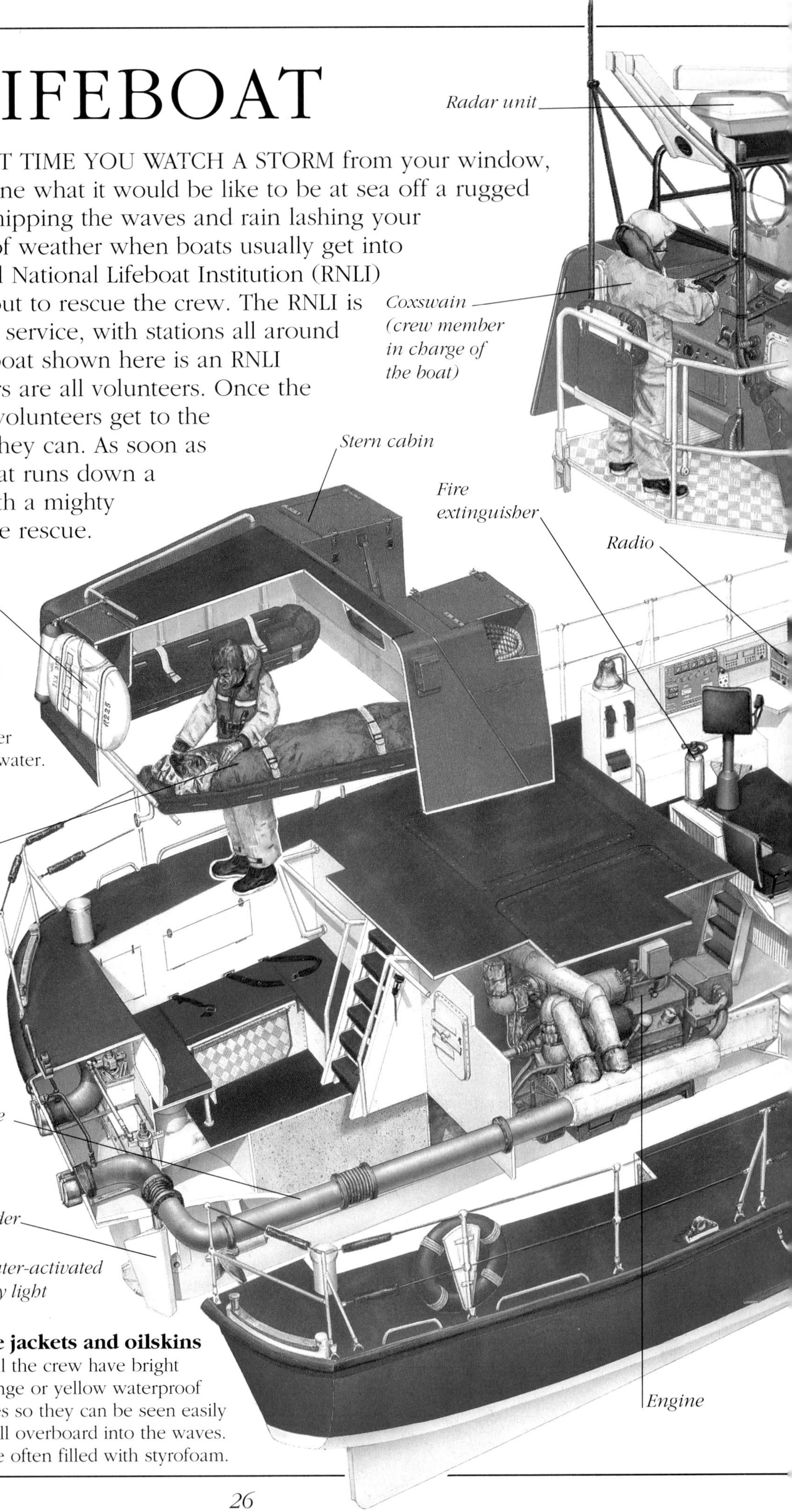

Radar unit

Coxswain (crew member in charge of the boat)

Stern cabin

Fire extinguisher

Radio

Emergency life raft

Skimming to the rescue
The Tyne Class has a lightweight steel hull that helps it travel fast. As the boat gathers speed, it planes, which means it skims over the sea surface partly out of the water.

Stretcher with casualty strapped in

Lifesaving list
There is a lot of rescue equipment on board. The list includes a line rocket, used to fire a rope across to another ship, and nets that can be hung over the side for people to climb up.

Whistle

Engine exhaust pipe

Reflective strip

Rudder

Seawater-activated battery light

Life jackets and oilskins
All the crew have bright orange or yellow waterproof clothes so they can be seen easily if they fall overboard into the waves. Life jackets are often filled with styrofoam.

Engine

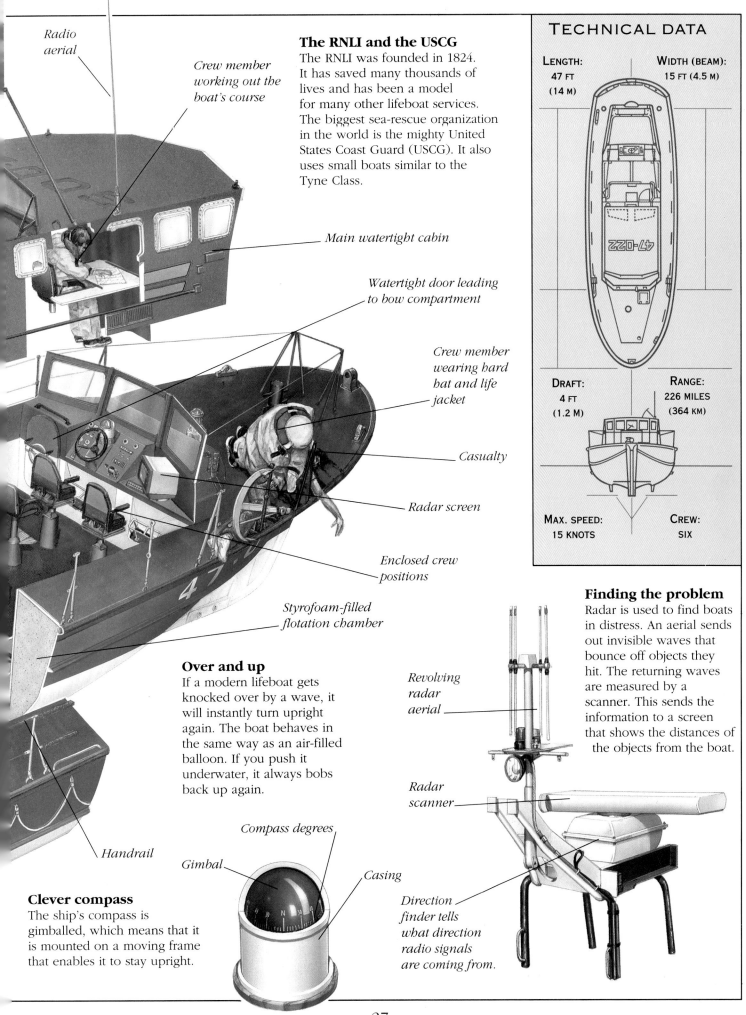

Radio aerial

Crew member working out the boat's course

The RNLI and the USCG

The RNLI was founded in 1824. It has saved many thousands of lives and has been a model for many other lifeboat services. The biggest sea-rescue organization in the world is the mighty United States Coast Guard (USCG). It also uses small boats similar to the Tyne Class.

Main watertight cabin

Watertight door leading to bow compartment

Crew member wearing hard hat and life jacket

Casualty

Radar screen

Enclosed crew positions

Styrofoam-filled flotation chamber

LENGTH:	WIDTH (BEAM):
47 FT (14 M)	15 FT (4.5 M)

DRAFT:	RANGE:
4 FT (1.2 M)	226 MILES (364 KM)

MAX. SPEED:	CREW:
15 KNOTS	SIX

Over and up

If a modern lifeboat gets knocked over by a wave, it will instantly turn upright again. The boat behaves in the same way as an air-filled balloon. If you push it underwater, it always bobs back up again.

Finding the problem

Radar is used to find boats in distress. An aerial sends out invisible waves that bounce off objects they hit. The returning waves are measured by a scanner. This sends the information to a screen that shows the distances of the objects from the boat.

Revolving radar aerial

Radar scanner

Handrail

Compass degrees

Gimbal

Casing

Direction finder tells what direction radio signals are coming from.

Clever compass

The ship's compass is gimballed, which means that it is mounted on a moving frame that enables it to stay upright.

NAUTICAL TIMELINE

THE HISTORY of shipbuilding stretches back thousands of years. The first boats were made from inflated skins, hollowed-out logs, or bundles of reeds tied together. Since that time, ship design has changed gradually but dramatically, and it is still changing today. Here are some milestones in the development of the modern vessel.

INFLATED ANIMAL SKINS

REED BOAT

Reed bundles

C. AD 800 VIKING LONGSHIP

C. 1200 CHINESE JUNK

C. 1250 MEDIEVAL COG

Rudder

Steering oar

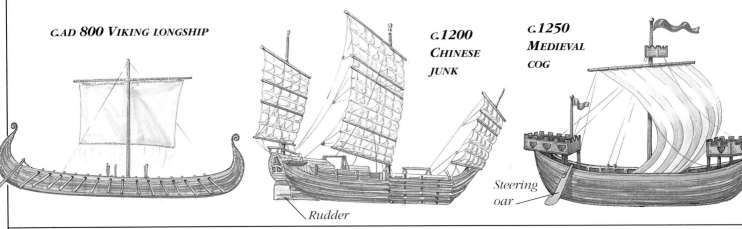

C. 1800 100-GUN MAN-OF-WAR

1843 IRON-HULLED SCREW STEAMER SS GREAT BRITAIN

Funnel

Iron hull

Propeller

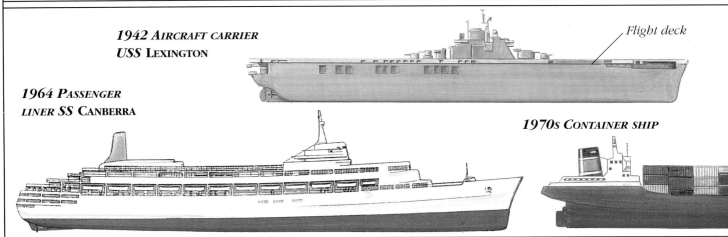

1942 AIRCRAFT CARRIER USS LEXINGTON

Flight deck

1964 PASSENGER LINER SS CANBERRA

1970S CONTAINER SHIP

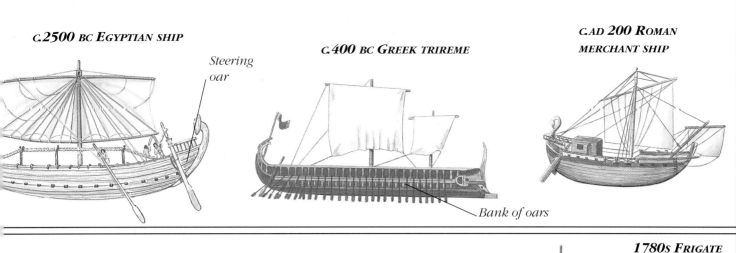

c.2500 bc Egyptian ship

Steering oar

c.400 bc Greek trireme

Bank of oars

c.ad 200 Roman merchant ship

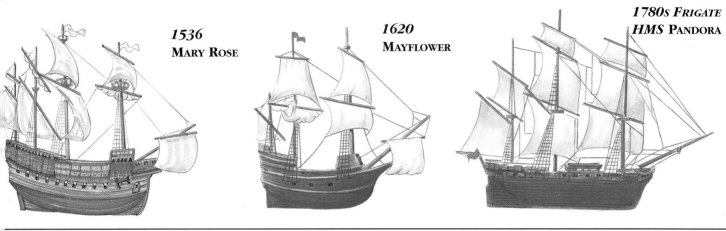

1536 Mary Rose

1620 Mayflower

1780s Frigate HMS Pandora

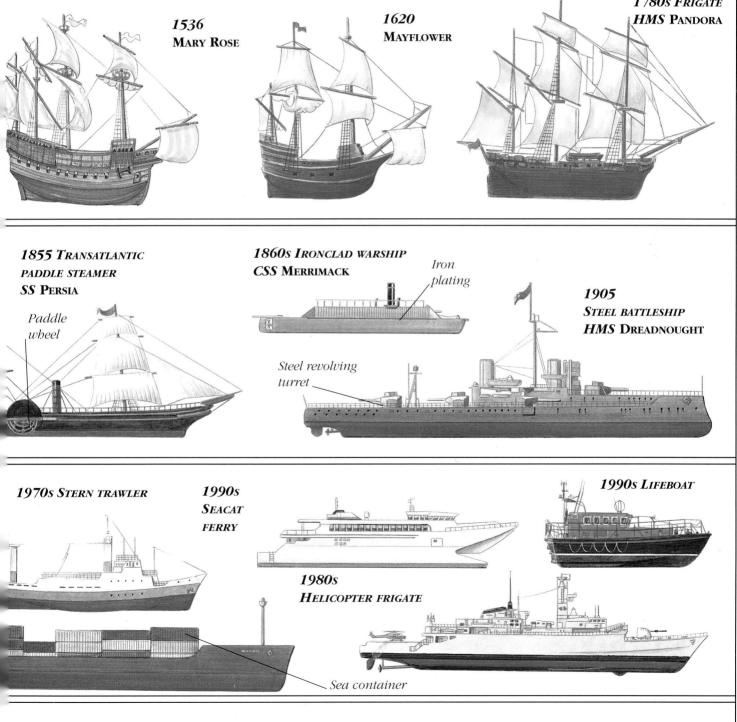

1855 Transatlantic paddle steamer SS Persia

Paddle wheel

1860s Ironclad warship CSS Merrimack

Iron plating

Steel revolving turret

1905 Steel battleship HMS Dreadnought

1970s Stern trawler

1990s Seacat ferry

1990s Lifeboat

1980s Helicopter frigate

Sea container

GLOSSARY

Aft
The area that is near or toward the back (stern) of a ship.

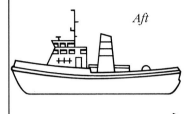

Aft

Amidships
The area in the middle of a ship.

Anchor
A heavy weight on the end of a rope or thick chain. It is thrown over the side and sticks in the seabed to stop a ship from drifting. When a ship is "anchored," it is stationary.

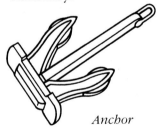

Anchor

Ballast
Weighty pieces of stone or cargo loaded into the bottom part of a ship to help balance it in water.

Bilge pump
A pump used to get rid of water that might have leaked inside a ship. A pump is usually placed on either side of the keel, in the broadest part of the hold at the bottom of a ship. This area is called the bilge.

Boatswain
The foreman of a boat crew (usually shortened to Bo'sun).

Boiler
A watertight container where water is turned into steam.

Bow
The front of a ship.

Bowsprit
A long spar sticking out from the front of a sailing ship. A bowsprit sail hangs here.

Bridge
An enclosed platform from which the captain and helmsman navigate a ship. Orders are given from here.

Broadside
A volley of gunfire from one side of a ship.

Bulkhead
An inner wall that divides a ship into watertight sections.

Bulwark
The top part of the hull that runs around a ship above the upper deck.

Cabin
Living quarters for someone on board.

Capstan
A winding machine used to haul up heavy loads such as the anchor.

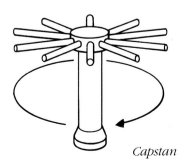

Capstan

Carvel built
A wooden hull made of planks laid tightly edge to edge.

Clinker built
A wooden hull made of overlapping planks.

Compass
An instrument with a magnetic needle that always points north.

Deck
A platform that stretches across and along a boat.

Forecastle
(usually shortened to fo'c'sle) A raised fighting platform at the front of a wooden ship. In a modern ship, it is the area where the crew cabins are usually found.

Foremast
The mast situated in front of the mainmast.

Forward
Toward the front of the boat.

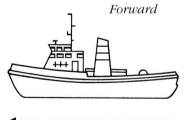

Forward

Frigate
A small warship.

Funnel
A large pipe used on steamships to carry smoke and steam up from a ship's engines. It is open to the sky at the top.

Galley
A ship's kitchen. Also, a boat powered by rows of oarsmen.

Gunport
A hole cut in the side of a ship so that a gun, such as a cannon, can fire out.

Helmsman
The person who steers a ship.

Hold
The space inside the bottom of a ship. It is often used for storing cargo and provisions.

Hull
The outer shell of a ship.

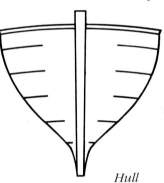

Hull

Junk
A Chinese boat with bamboo-ribbed sails.

Keel
A strong rib that runs all the way along the bottom of the hull. It is the backbone of a ship.

Knot
The measure of a ship's speed. One knot is one nautical mile per hour.

Mainmast
The pole stretching up from the deck in the middle of a sailing ship.

Man-of-War
A large, heavily-armed sailing warship of the 18th and 19th centuries.

Mate
A ship's officer, ranked beneath the captain.

Merchant ship
A ship used for carrying cargo, not for fighting.

Mizzenmast
The mast situated behind the mainmast.

Outrigger
An extension, built so that it sticks out from the side of a boat's hull.

Poop deck
A high deck raised above the stern (back) of a ship.

Port
The left-hand side of a ship. It is also an order that means "turn to the left."

Propeller
Blades mounted on a shaft underneath the water at the back of a ship. It is also called a screw. A ship's engines drive it around in the water, pushing the ship forward.

Propeller

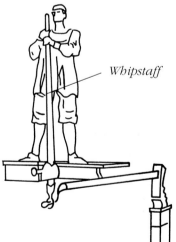

Prow
The part of a hull that sticks out at the very front of a wooden ship.

Quarterdeck
The raised deck at the rear of a sailing ship.

Radar
A revolving aerial that sends out invisible electromagnetic waves, which bounce off any objects they hit. The returning waves are measured by a radar scanner, and the measurements show how far away the objects are. Sailors use radar to find other ships.

Ram
A long, pointed projection at the front of a wooden ship, located underneath the water. It was used to sink enemy ships by ramming holes into them below the waterline.

Rigging
Ropes or wires used to hold up the sails and masts on a sailing ship.

Rudder
A large piece of timber or metal hinged to a post that fits into a ship at the back. The rudder is moved to the left or right to make a ship change direction.

Sail
A large sheet of canvas, carried on the masts of a sailing ship, used to harness the wind's power to drive the ship forward. Sails are identified by the mast on which they are carried.

Sail

Shipwright
A shipbuilder.

Starboard
The right-hand side of a ship. It is also an order that means "turn to the right."

Stem
The narrowest part at the front extremity of a ship, which parts the water as the ship moves forward.

Stern
The back of a ship.

Tiller
A part inside a boat that is attached to the rudder outside. When the tiller is moved, the rudder moves.

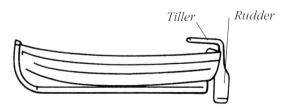

Tiller   *Rudder*

Trireme
An ancient Greek boat powered by three rows of oarsmen.

Waterline
The water level along the side of a ship.

Wheel
The ship's wheel is turned to move the rudder and steer the vessel.

Wheel

Whipstaff
A giant lever attached to the tiller on an old wooden ship. Before ships had steering wheels, the sailors swung the whipstaff to make the rudder move.

Whipstaff

Yard
A long pole that goes across a mast from which sails are hung. Small sailboats have one yard; large ships have several.

INDEX

A

aircraft carrier, 18-21
anchor, stockless, 24
anti-aircraft (AA) guns, 18
archers, 9
armor plating, 14, 21
arrestor cables, 21

B

battleship, 14-15
HMS *Bounty*, 12-13
bulkheads, 23

C

SS *Canberra*, 16-17
cannons, 8
captain, 13, 17
carrack, 8
carriage guns, 8
carronades, 13
carvel planking, 8
castles, 8
cell, 13
Chinese junk, 22-23
clinker planking, 8
compass, 27
crewmen, 12, 17

D

decks, 12, 17;
      see also flight deck,
      hangar deck
HMS *Dreadnought*, 14-15

E

engines, *see* steam turbine
      engines
eye, painted, 6, 22

F

fighting tops, 8
figurehead, 12
fire director
      HMS *Dreadnought*, 15

USS *Lexington*, 19, 20
fish-washing machine, 25
fishing boat, 24-25
fishing nets, 24, 25
flight deck, 18
forecastle (fo'c'sle), 8, 12
frigate, 12

G

gimballed compass, 27
gun sighting device, *see*
      fire director
gun turret, 21
gunports, 8
guns
      HMS *Dreadnought* , 15
      USS *Lexington*, 18, 21
      Mary Rose, 8-9
      Mayflower, 11
      HMS *Pandora*, 12, 13

H

hangar deck, 19
house, 23
hull, 16, 26
hypozoma, 7

I

island, 19; *see also*
      superstructure

J

junk, 22-23

K

Kamikaze suicide
      planes, 18

L

USS *Lexington*, 18-21
life jackets, 26
life rocket, 26
lifeboats, 16, 26-27

M

Mary Rose, 8-9
masts
      Mary Rose, 8
      Mayflower, 10
      trireme, 6
Mayflower, 10-11
merchant ship, 10-11

N

nets/netting
      HMS *Dreadnought*, 14
      lifeboat, 26
      Mary Rose, 9
      trawler, 24, 25

O

oarsmen, 6
ocean liner, 16-17
officers, 13
oilskins, 26
otter boards, 25

P

HMS *Pandora*, 12-13
passenger cabins, 16
pilgrims, 10-11
pinnace, 14
planking, 8
prisoners, 13
propellers, 16

Q

quarterdeck, 13

R

radar, 20, 27
radio aerials, 20
ram, 6
RNLI, 26, 27
rudder, 22, 23

S

sails
      Mayflower, 10
      trireme, 6
soldiers, 9
steam catapult, 18
steam pinnace, 14
steam turbine engines
      SS *Canberra*, 16
      HMS *Dreadnought*, 14
      USS *Lexington*, 20
stern trawler, 24
sterncastle, 8
stockless anchor, 24
superstructure, 17; *see
      also* island

T

toilets, 10
torpedoes, 14
trawl, 24
trawler, 24-25
trireme, 6-7

W

warships
      USS *Lexington*, 18-21
      Mary Rose, 8-9
      HMS *Pandora*, 12-13
watertight compartments, 21,
      22, 23
weapons, 9; *see also* guns
whipstaff, 11

Acknowledgments

Dorling Kindersley would like
to thank the following people
who helped in the preparation
of this book:

Constance Novis for editorial
support
Lynn Bresler for the index
Additional artwork by Chris Lyon
(page 14-15, 18-21) Roger Stewart
(page 16-17) and Brihton
Illustration (page 28-29)
Line artworks by John See